To my beloved wife, whose unwavering love and support are the inspiration behind all of my achievements. With your kindness, patience, and constant encouragement, you make each day brighter and more meaningful. May this book serve as a small reflection of the brightness and joy you bring into my life. Thank you for being my greatest source of inspiration and for sharing this journey with me. With all my love and gratitude, this book is for you.

Vanderlei Santos

Digital Corpore

2024

THIS BOOK BELONGS TO

____

Vanderlei Santos

Digital Corpore

2024

SPACE TO TEST YOUR COLOR

SPACE TO TEST YOUR COLOR

SPACE TO TEST YOUR COLOR

SPACE TO TEST YOUR COLOR

SPACE TO TEST YOUR COLOR

SPACE TO TEST YOUR COLOR

SPACE TO TEST YOUR COLOR

SPACE TO TEST YOUR COLOR

SPACE TO TEST YOUR COLOR

SPACE TO TEST YOUR COLOR

SPACE TO TEST YOUR COLOR

SPACE TO TEST YOUR COLOR

SPACE TO TEST YOUR COLOR

SPACE TO TEST YOUR COLOR

SPACE TO TEST YOUR COLOR

SPACE TO TEST YOUR COLOR

SPACE TO TEST YOUR COLOR

SPACE TO TEST YOUR COLOR

SPACE TO TEST YOUR COLOR

SPACE TO TEST YOUR COLOR

SPACE TO TEST YOUR COLOR

SPACE TO TEST YOUR COLOR

SPACE TO TEST YOUR COLOR

SPACE TO TEST YOUR COLOR

SPACE TO TEST YOUR COLOR

SPACE TO TEST YOUR COLOR

SPACE TO TEST YOUR COLOR

SPACE TO TEST YOUR COLOR

SPACE TO TEST YOUR COLOR

SPACE TO TEST YOUR COLOR

SPACE TO TEST YOUR COLOR

SPACE TO TEST YOUR COLOR

SPACE TO TEST YOUR COLOR

SPACE TO TEST YOUR COLOR

SPACE TO TEST YOUR COLOR

SPACE TO TEST YOUR COLOR

SPACE TO TEST YOUR COLOR

SPACE TO TEST YOUR COLOR

SPACE TO TEST YOUR COLOR

SPACE TO TEST YOUR COLOR

SPACE TO TEST YOUR COLOR

SPACE TO TEST YOUR COLOR

SPACE TO TEST YOUR COLOR

SPACE TO TEST YOUR COLOR

SPACE TO TEST YOUR COLOR

SPACE TO TEST YOUR COLOR

SPACE TO TEST YOUR COLOR

SPACE TO TEST YOUR COLOR

SPACE TO TEST YOUR COLOR

SPACE TO TEST YOUR COLOR

SPACE TO TEST YOUR COLOR

SPACE TO TEST YOUR COLOR

SPACE TO TEST YOUR COLOR

SPACE TO TEST YOUR COLOR

SPACE TO TEST YOUR COLOR

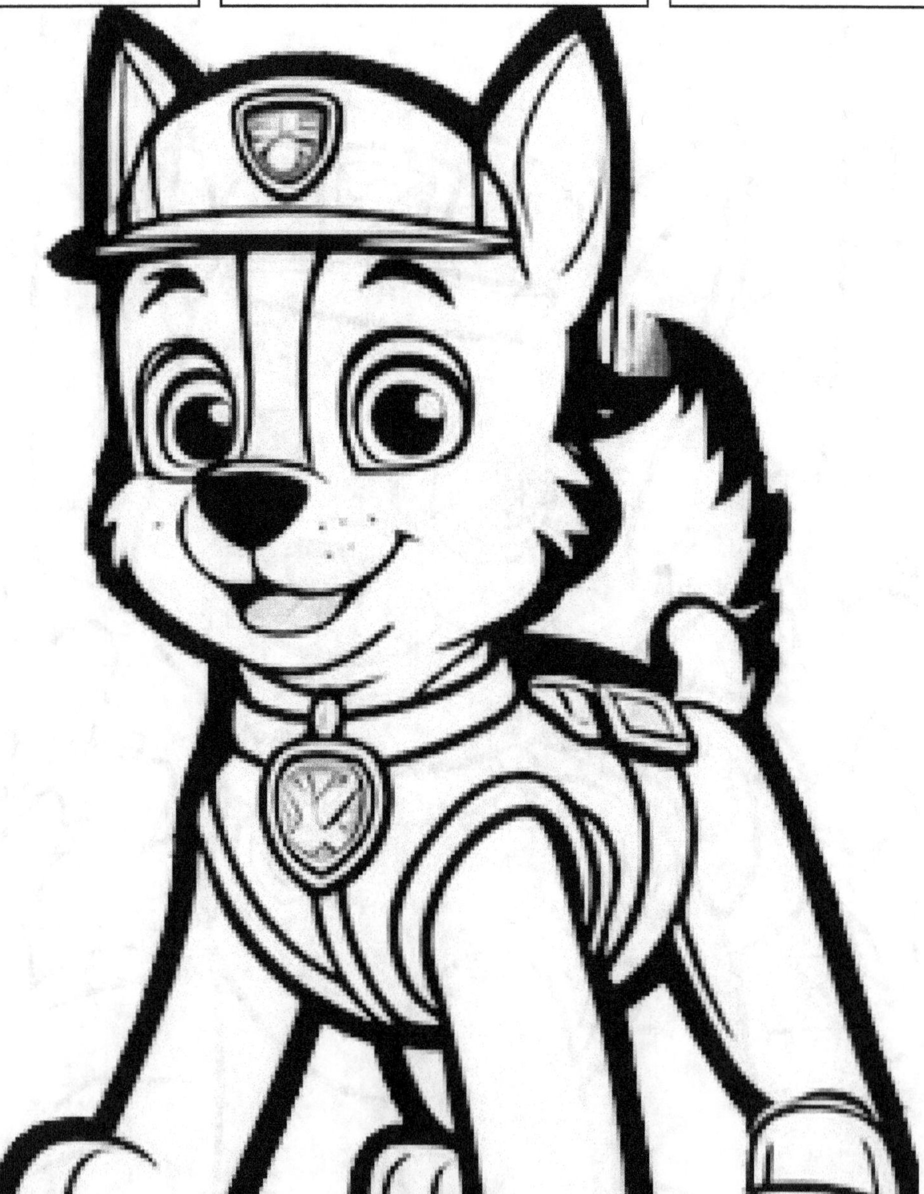

SPACE TO TEST YOUR COLOR

SPACE TO TEST YOUR COLOR

SPACE TO TEST YOUR COLOR

SPACE TO TEST YOUR COLOR

SPACE TO TEST YOUR COLOR

SPACE TO TEST YOUR COLOR

SPACE TO TEST YOUR COLOR

SPACE TO TEST YOUR COLOR

SPACE TO TEST YOUR COLOR

SPACE TO TEST YOUR COLOR

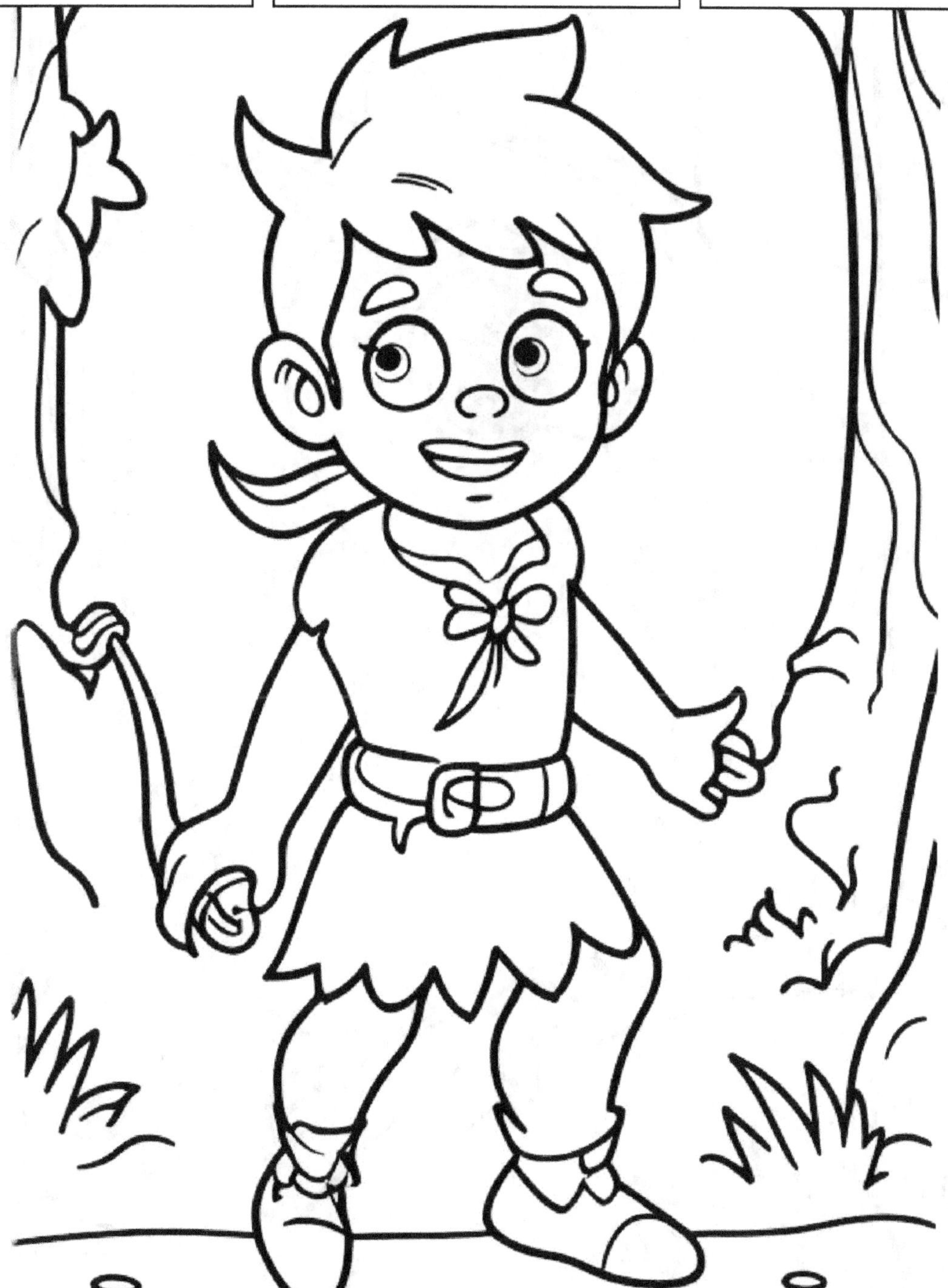

SPACE TO TEST YOUR COLOR

SPACE TO TEST YOUR COLOR

SPACE TO TEST YOUR COLOR

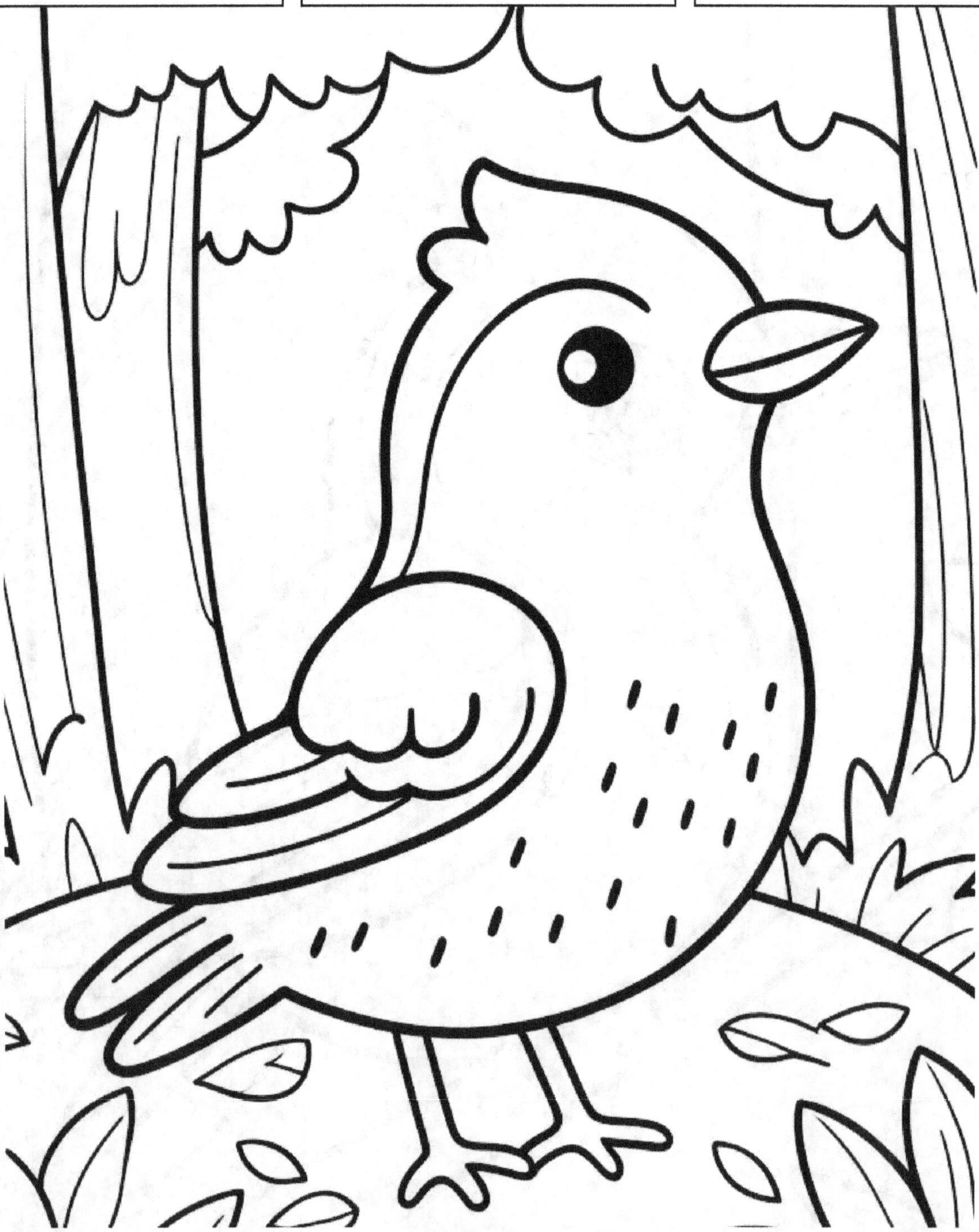

SPACE TO TEST YOUR COLOR

SPACE TO TEST YOUR COLOR

SPACE TO TEST YOUR COLOR

SPACE TO TEST YOUR COLOR

SPACE TO TEST YOUR COLOR

SPACE TO TEST YOUR COLOR

SPACE TO TEST YOUR COLOR

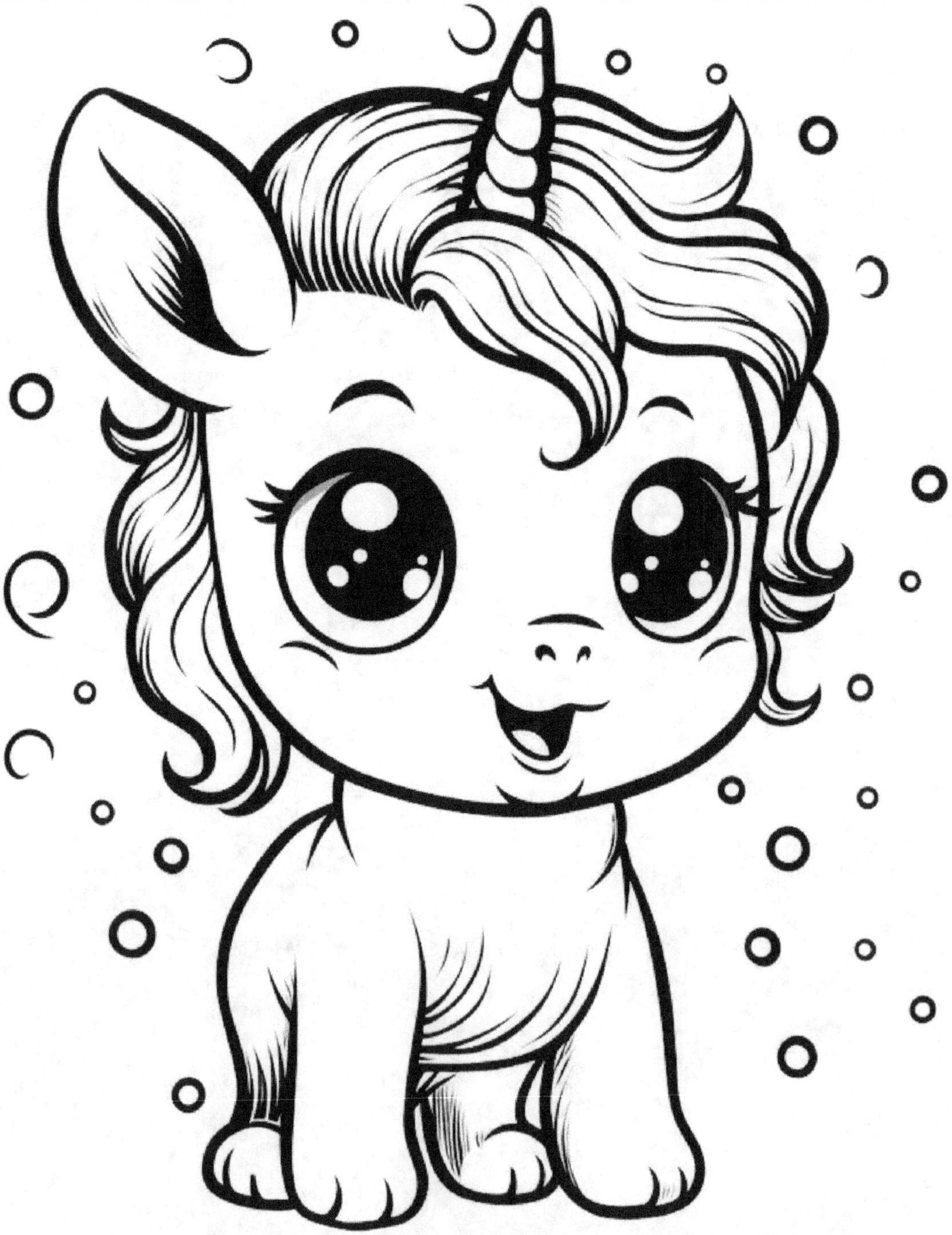

SPACE TO TEST YOUR COLOR

SPACE TO TEST YOUR COLOR

SPACE TO TEST YOUR COLOR

SPACE TO TEST YOUR COLOR

SPACE TO TEST YOUR COLOR

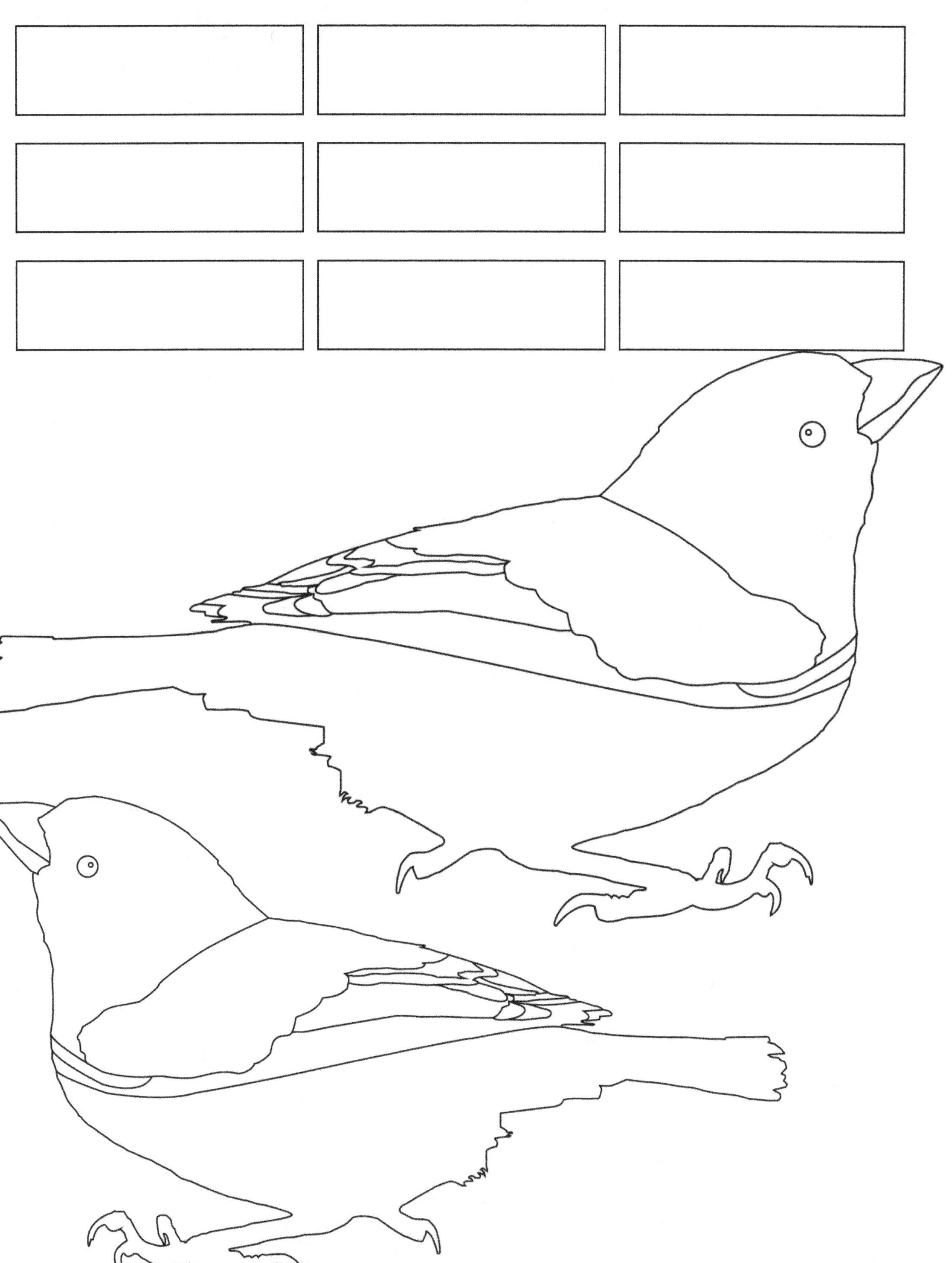

SPACE TO TEST YOUR COLOR

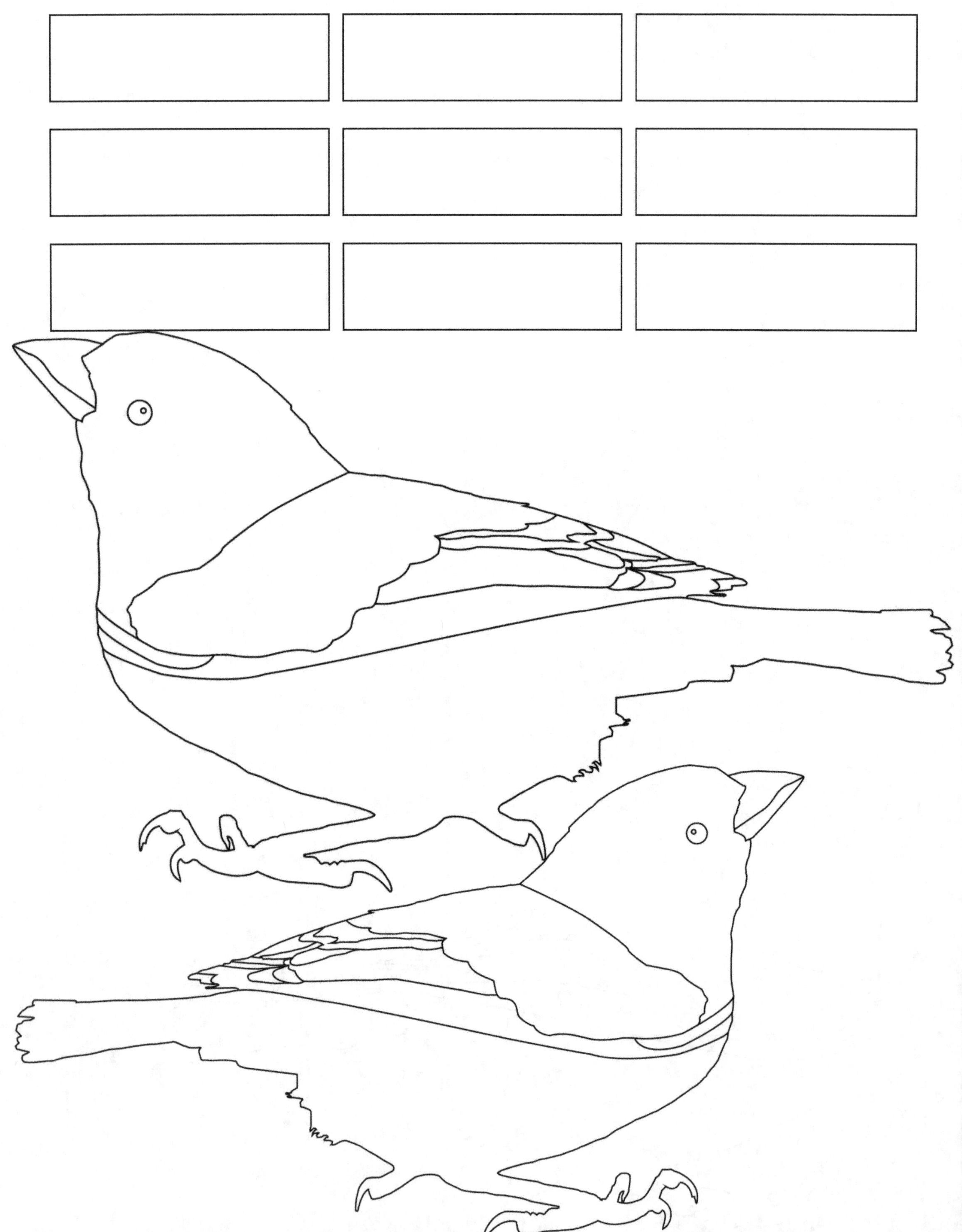

SPACE TO TEST YOUR COLOR

SPACE TO TEST YOUR COLOR

SPACE TO TEST YOUR COLOR

SPACE TO TEST YOUR COLOR

SPACE TO TEST YOUR COLOR

SPACE TO TEST YOUR COLOR

SPACE TO TEST YOUR COLOR

SPACE TO TEST YOUR COLOR

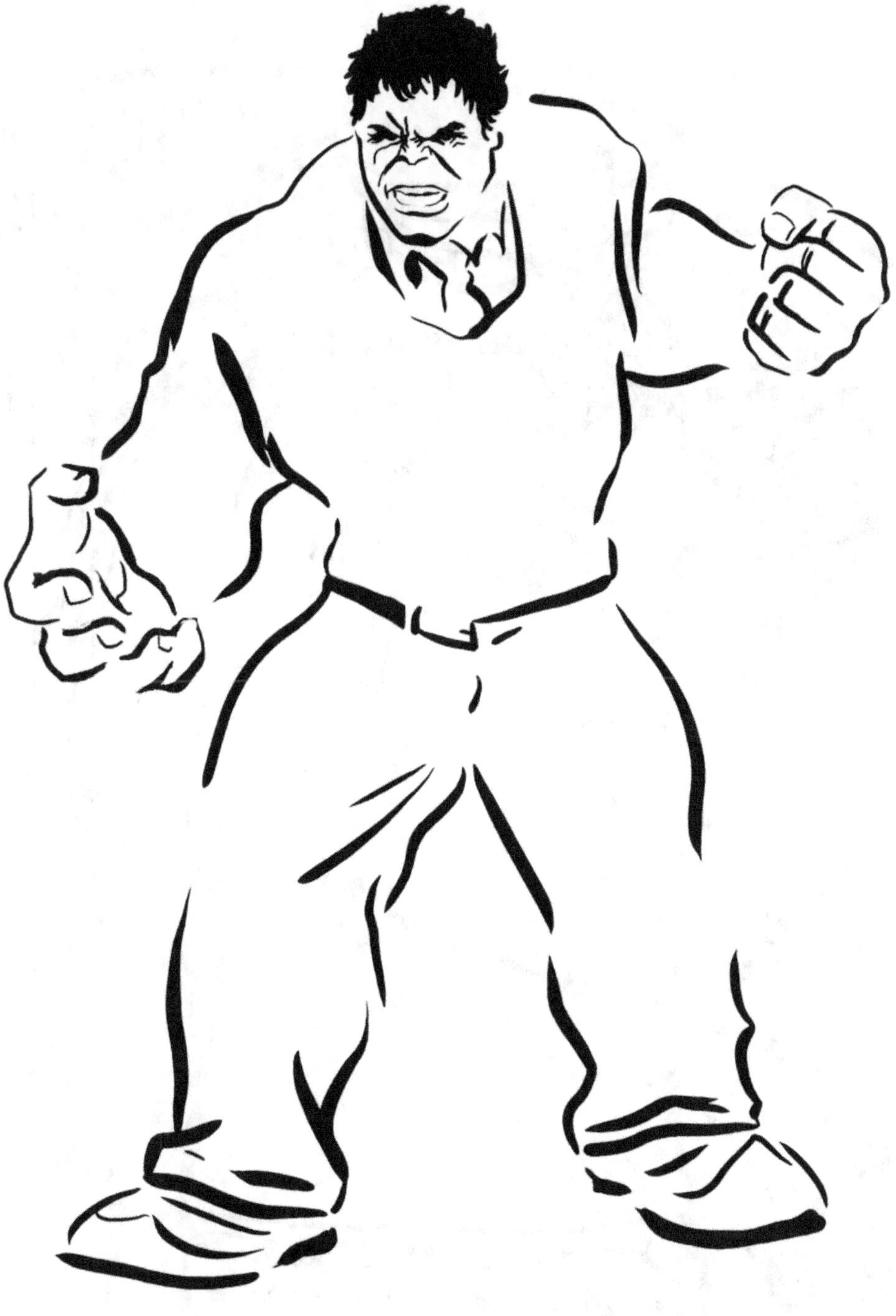

SPACE TO TEST YOUR COLOR

SPACE TO TEST YOUR COLOR

SPACE TO TEST YOUR COLOR

SPACE TO TEST YOUR COLOR

SPACE TO TEST YOUR COLOR

SPACE TO TEST YOUR COLOR

SPACE TO TEST YOUR COLOR

SPACE TO TEST YOUR COLOR

SPACE TO TEST YOUR COLOR

SPACE TO TEST YOUR COLOR

MOTHER

SPACE TO TEST YOUR COLOR

SPACE TO TEST YOUR COLOR

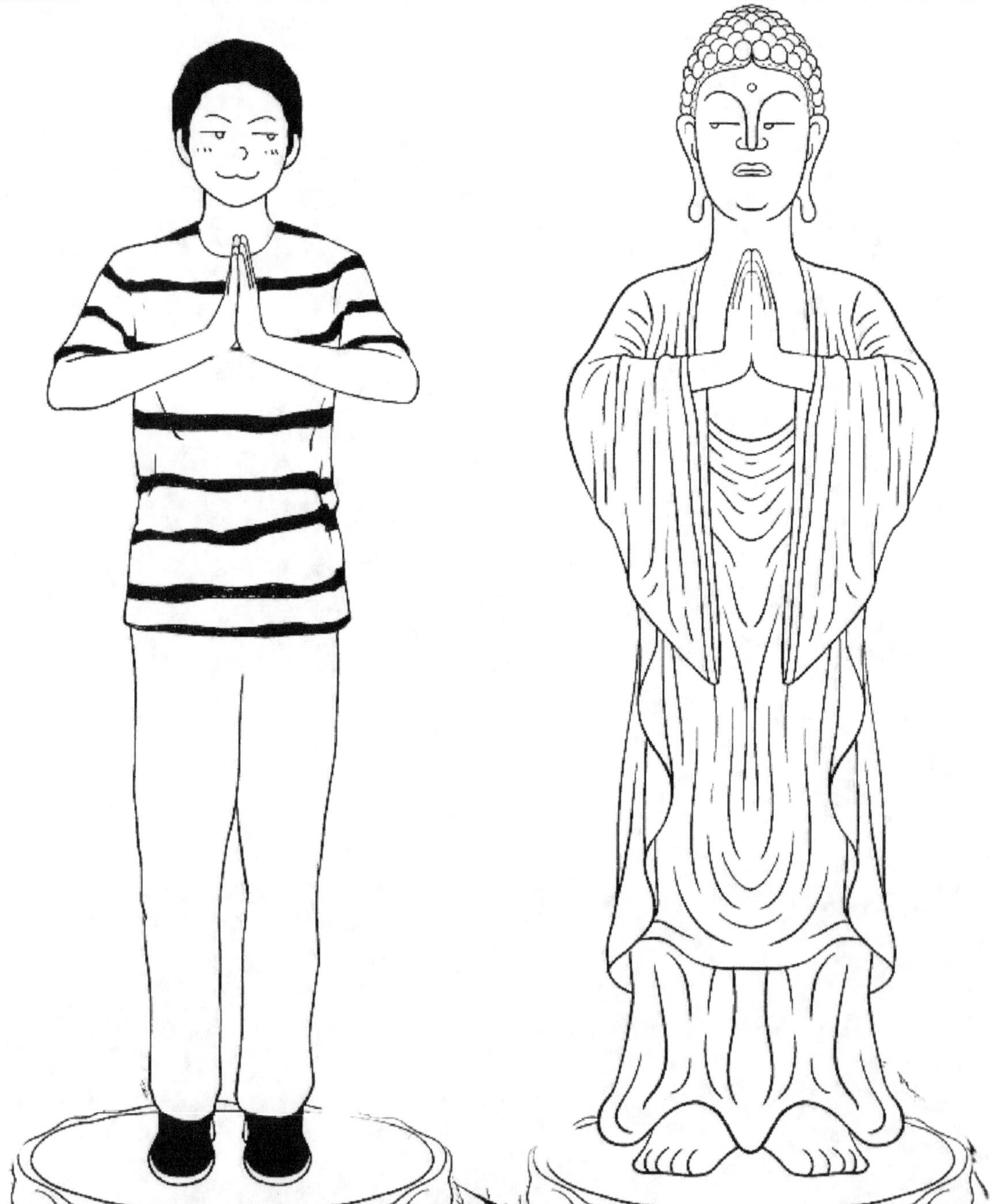

SPACE TO TEST YOUR COLOR

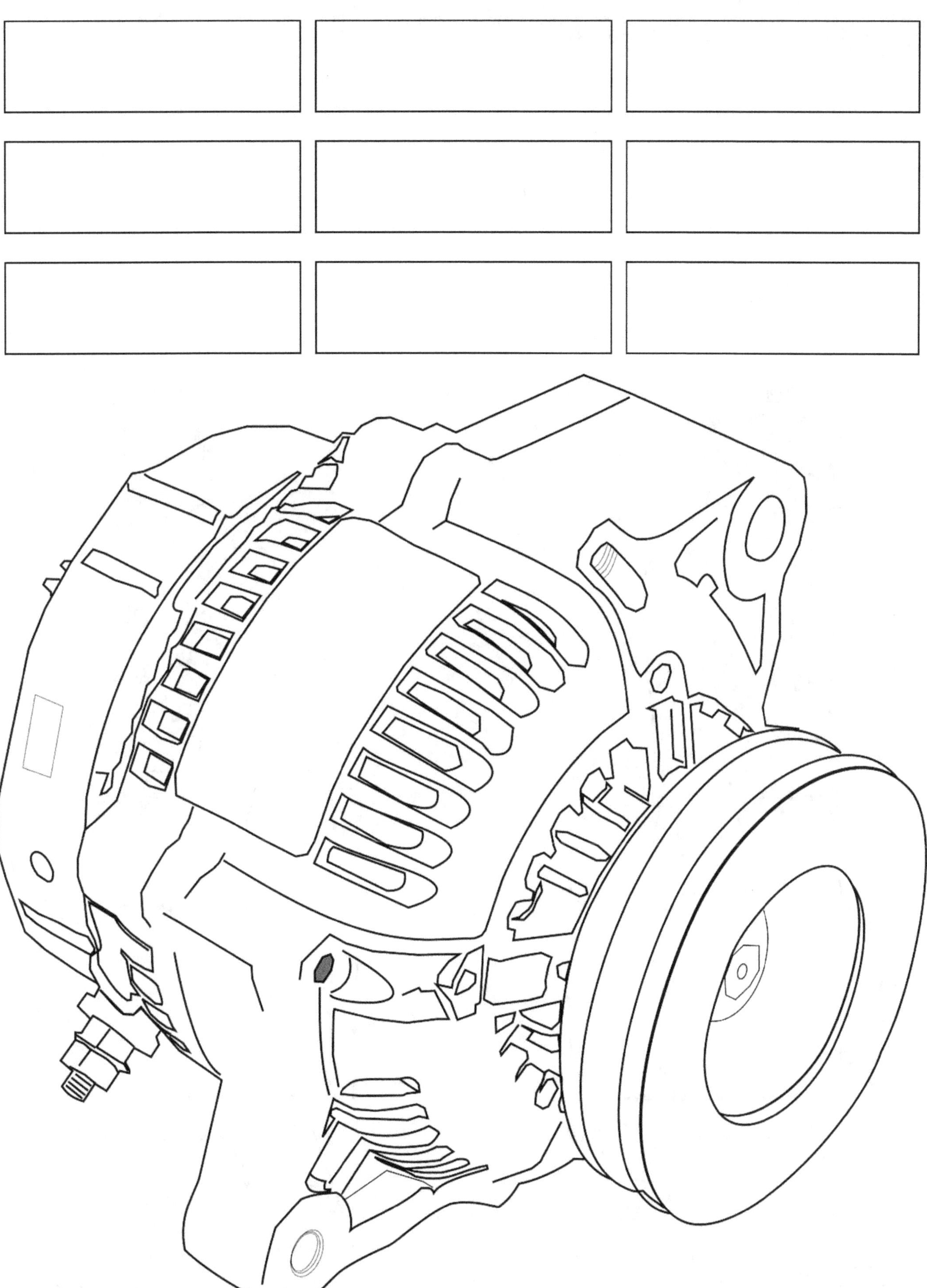

SPACE TO TEST YOUR COLOR

SPACE TO TEST YOUR COLOR

SPACE TO TEST YOUR COLOR

SPACE TO TEST YOUR COLOR

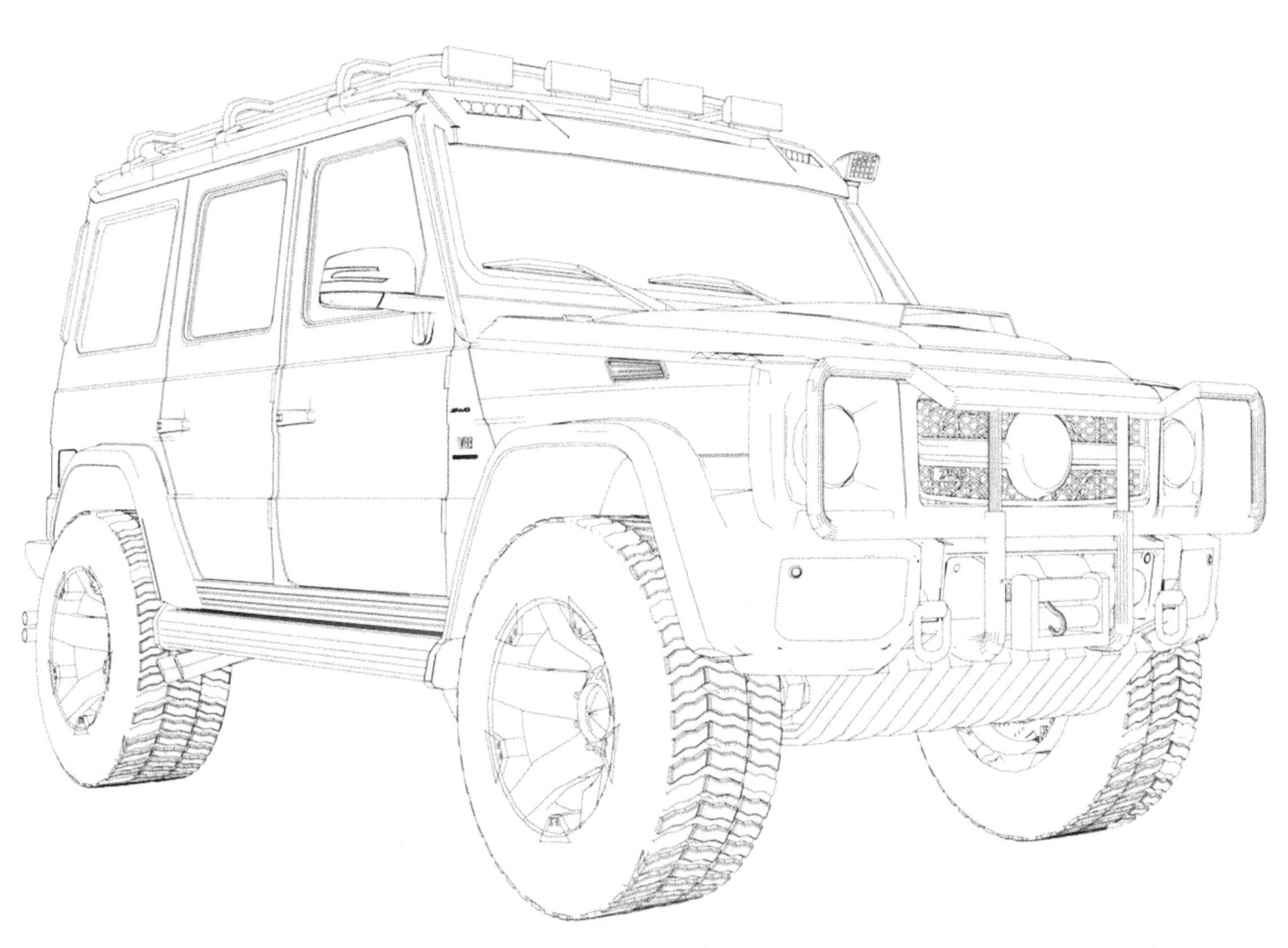

SPACE TO TEST YOUR COLOR

SPACE TO TEST YOUR COLOR

SPACE TO TEST YOUR COLOR

SPACE TO TEST YOUR COLOR

SPACE TO TEST YOUR COLOR

SPACE TO TEST YOUR COLOR

SPACE TO TEST YOUR COLOR

SPACE TO TEST YOUR COLOR

SPACE TO TEST YOUR COLOR

SPACE TO TEST YOUR COLOR

SPACE TO TEST YOUR COLOR

SPACE TO TEST YOUR COLOR

SPACE TO TEST YOUR COLOR

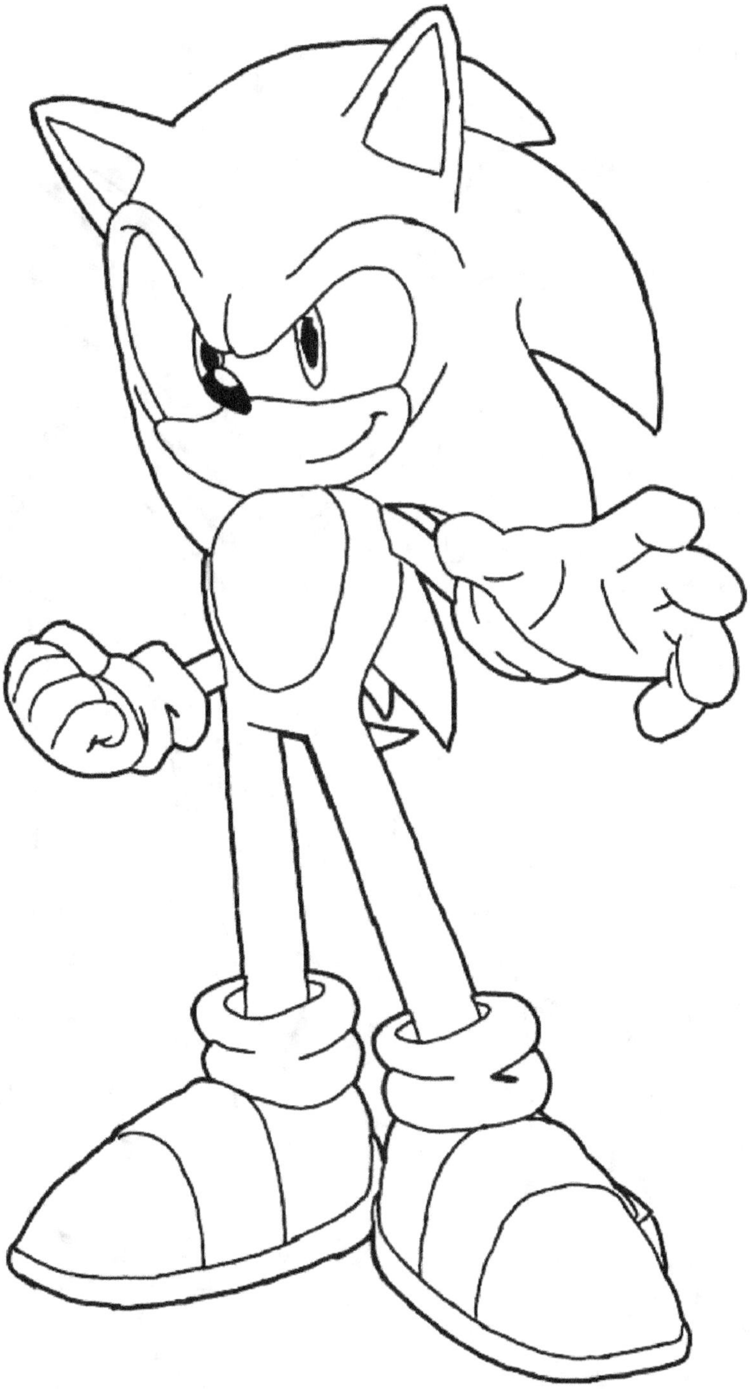

SPACE TO TEST YOUR COLOR

SPACE TO TEST YOUR COLOR

SPACE TO TEST YOUR COLOR

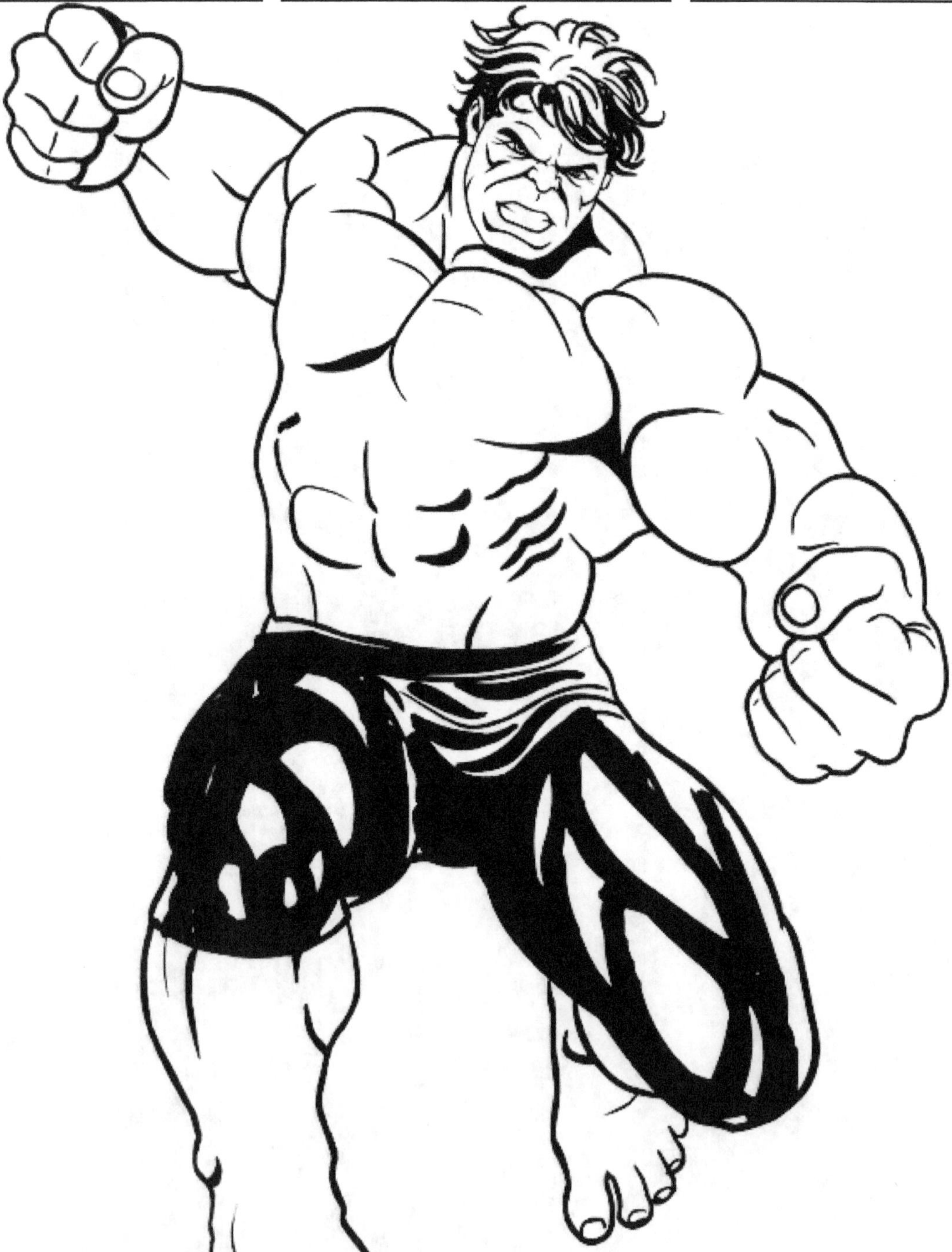

SPACE TO TEST YOUR COLOR

SPACE TO TEST YOUR COLOR

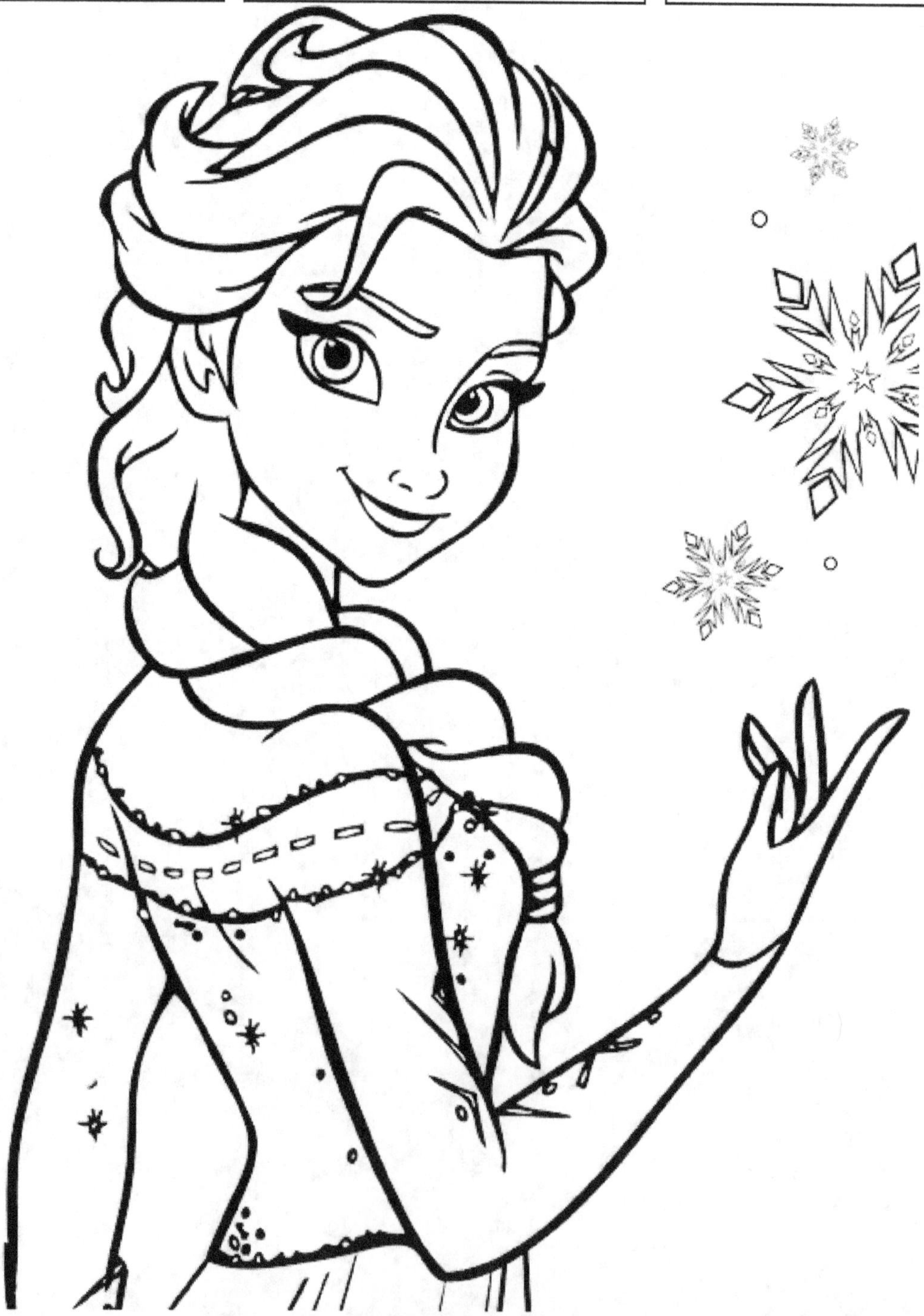

SPACE TO TEST YOUR COLOR

SPACE TO TEST YOUR COLOR

SPACE TO TEST YOUR COLOR

SPACE TO TEST YOUR COLOR

www.ingramcontent.com/pod-product-compliance
Lightning Source LLC
Chambersburg PA
CBHW080852250726
48663CB00004B/442